GUESTS

Name: _____

Address: _____

_____

Relationship To Parents: _____

BABY PREDICTIONS

Date Of Birth: _____

Time Of Birth: _____

Baby Weight: _____

Baby Height: _____

Hair Color: _____

Eye Color: _____

First Word: _____

Resemblance: ☐ Mom ☐ Dad

I Hope The Baby Gets Dad's

_____

_____

I Hope The Baby Gets Mom's

_____

_____

WISHES FOR BABY

_____

_____

_____

ADVICE FOR PARENTS

_____

_____

_____

Thanks For Sharing

GUESTS

Name: _____

Address: _____

_____

Relationship To Parents: _____

BABY PREDICTIONS

Date Of Birth: _____

Time Of Birth: _____

Baby Weight: _____

Baby Height: _____

Hair Color: _____

Eye Color: _____

First Word: _____

Resemblance: ☐ Mom ☐ Dad

I Hope The Baby Gets Dad's

_____

_____

I Hope The Baby Gets Mom's

_____

_____

WISHES FOR BABY

_____

_____

_____

ADVICE FOR PARENTS

_____

_____

_____

Thanks For Sharing

GUESTS

Name: _____

Address: _____

_____

Relationship To Parents: _____

BABY PREDICTIONS

Date Of Birth: _____

Time Of Birth: _____

Baby Weight: _____

Baby Height: _____

Hair Color: _____

Eye Color: _____

First Word: _____

Resemblance: ☐ Mom ☐ Dad

I Hope The Baby Gets Dad's

_____

I Hope The Baby Gets Mom's

_____

WISHES FOR BABY

_____

_____

_____

ADVICE FOR PARENTS

_____

_____

Thanks For Sharing

GUESTS

Name: _____

Address: _____

_____

Relationship To Parents: _____

BABY PREDICTIONS

Date Of Birth: _____

Time Of Birth: _____

Baby Weight: _____

Baby Height: _____

Hair Color: _____

Eye Color: _____

First Word: _____

Resemblance: ☐ Mom ☐ Dad

I Hope The Baby Gets Dad's

_____

_____

I Hope The Baby Gets Mom's

_____

_____

WISHES FOR BABY

_____

_____

_____

ADVICE FOR PARENTS

_____

_____

_____

Thanks For Sharing

GUESTS

Name: _____

Address: _____

_____

Relationship To Parents: _____

BABY PREDICTIONS

Date Of Birth: _____

Time Of Birth: _____

Baby Weight: _____

Baby Height: _____

Hair Color: _____

Eye Color: _____

First Word: _____

Resemblance: ☐ Mom ☐ Dad

I Hope The Baby Gets Dad's

_____

_____

I Hope The Baby Gets Mom's

_____

_____

WISHES FOR BABY

_____

_____

_____

ADVICE FOR PARENTS

_____

_____

Thanks For Sharing

GUESTS

Name: _____

Address: _____

_____

Relationship To Parents: _____

BABY PREDICTIONS

Date Of Birth: _____

Time Of Birth: _____

Baby Weight: _____

Baby Height: _____

Hair Color: _____

Eye Color: _____

First Word: _____

Resemblance: ☐ Mom ☐ Dad

I Hope The Baby Gets Dad's

_____

I Hope The Baby Gets Mom's

_____

WISHES FOR BABY

_____

_____

_____

ADVICE FOR PARENTS

_____

_____

_____

Thanks For Sharing

GUESTS

Name: _____

Address: _____

_____

Relationship To Parents: _____

BABY PREDICTIONS

Date Of Birth: _____

Time Of Birth: _____

Baby Weight: _____

Baby Height: _____

Hair Color: _____

Eye Color: _____

First Word: _____

Resemblance: □ Mom □ Dad

I Hope The Baby Gets Dad's

_____

I Hope The Baby Gets Mom's

_____

WISHES FOR BABY

_____

_____

_____

ADVICE FOR PARENTS

_____

_____

_____

Thanks For Sharing

GUESTS

Name: _____

Address: _____

_____

Relationship To Parents: _____

BABY PREDICTIONS

Date Of Birth: _____

Time Of Birth: _____

Baby Weight: _____

Baby Height: _____

Hair Color: _____

Eye Color: _____

First Word: _____

Resemblance: ☐ Mom ☐ Dad

I Hope The Baby Gets Dad's

_____

_____

I Hope The Baby Gets Mom's

_____

_____

WISHES FOR BABY

_____

_____

_____

ADVICE FOR PARENTS

_____

_____

Thanks For Sharing

GUESTS

Name: _____

Address: _____

_____

Relationship To Parents: _____

BABY PREDICTIONS

Date Of Birth: _____

Time Of Birth: _____

Baby Weight: _____

Baby Height: _____

Hair Color: _____

Eye Color: _____

First Word: _____

Resemblance: ☐ Mom ☐ Dad

I Hope The Baby Gets Dad's

_____

_____

I Hope The Baby Gets Mom's

_____

_____

WISHES FOR BABY

_____

_____

_____

ADVICE FOR PARENTS

_____

_____

_____

Thanks For Sharing

GUESTS

Name: _____

Address: _____

_____

Relationship To Parents: _____

BABY PREDICTIONS

Date Of Birth: _____

Time Of Birth: _____

Baby Weight: _____

Baby Height: _____

Hair Color: _____

Eye Color: _____

First Word: _____

Resemblance: ☐ Mom ☐ Dad

I Hope The Baby Gets Dad's

_____

_____

I Hope The Baby Gets Mom's

_____

_____

WISHES FOR BABY

_____

_____

_____

ADVICE FOR PARENTS

_____

_____

Thanks For Sharing

GUESTS

Name: _____

Address: _____

_____

Relationship To Parents: _____

BABY PREDICTIONS

Date Of Birth: _____

Time Of Birth: _____

Baby Weight: _____

Baby Height: _____

Hair Color: _____

Eye Color: _____

First Word: _____

Resemblance: ☐ Mom ☐ Dad

I Hope The Baby Gets Dad's

_____

I Hope The Baby Gets Mom's

_____

WISHES FOR BABY

_____

_____

_____

ADVICE FOR PARENTS

_____

_____

Thanks For Sharing

GUESTS

Name: _____

Address: _____

_____

Relationship To Parents: _____

BABY PREDICTIONS

Date Of Birth: _____

Time Of Birth: _____

Baby Weight: _____

Baby Height: _____

Hair Color: _____

Eye Color: _____

First Word: _____

Resemblance: ☐ Mom ☐ Dad

I Hope The Baby Gets Dad's

_____

_____

I Hope The Baby Gets Mom's

_____

_____

WISHES FOR BABY

_____

_____

_____

ADVICE FOR PARENTS

_____

_____

_____

Thanks For Sharing

GUESTS

Name: _____

Address: _____

_____

Relationship To Parents: _____

BABY PREDICTIONS

Date Of Birth: _____

Time Of Birth: _____

Baby Weight: _____

Baby Height: _____

Hair Color: _____

Eye Color: _____

First Word: _____

Resemblance: ☐ Mom ☐ Dad

I Hope The Baby Gets Dad's

_____

I Hope The Baby Gets Mom's

_____

WISHES FOR BABY

_____

_____

_____

ADVICE FOR PARENTS

_____

_____

_____

Thanks For Sharing

GUESTS

Name: _____

Address: _____

_____

Relationship To Parents: _____

BABY PREDICTIONS

Date Of Birth: _____

Time Of Birth: _____

Baby Weight: _____

Baby Height: _____

Hair Color: _____

Eye Color: _____

First Word: _____

Resemblance: ☐ Mom ☐ Dad

I Hope The Baby Gets Dad's

_____

_____

I Hope The Baby Gets Mom's

_____

_____

WISHES FOR BABY

_____

_____

_____

ADVICE FOR PARENTS

_____

_____

_____

Thanks For Sharing

GUESTS

Name: _____

Address: _____

_____

Relationship To Parents: _____

BABY PREDICTIONS

Date Of Birth: _____

Time Of Birth: _____

Baby Weight: _____

Baby Height: _____

Hair Color: _____

Eye Color: _____

First Word: _____

Resemblance: ☐ Mom ☐ Dad

I Hope The Baby Gets Dad's

_____

_____

I Hope The Baby Gets Mom's

_____

_____

WISHES FOR BABY

_____

_____

_____

ADVICE FOR PARENTS

_____

_____

_____

Thanks For Sharing

GUESTS

Name: _____

Address: _____

_____

Relationship To Parents: _____

BABY PREDICTIONS

Date Of Birth: _____

Time Of Birth: _____

Baby Weight: _____

Baby Height: _____

Hair Color: _____

Eye Color: _____

First Word: _____

Resemblance: ☐ Mom ☐ Dad

I Hope The Baby Gets Dad's

_____

I Hope The Baby Gets Mom's

_____

WISHES FOR BABY

_____

_____

_____

ADVICE FOR PARENTS

_____

_____

_____

Thanks For Sharing

GUESTS

Name: _____

Address: _____

_____

Relationship To Parents: _____

BABY PREDICTIONS

Date Of Birth: _____

Time Of Birth: _____

Baby Weight: _____

Baby Height: _____

Hair Color: _____

Eye Color: _____

First Word: _____

Resemblance: ☐ Mom ☐ Dad

I Hope The Baby Gets Dad's

_____

_____

I Hope The Baby Gets Mom's

_____

_____

WISHES FOR BABY

_____

_____

_____

ADVICE FOR PARENTS

_____

_____

Thanks For Sharing

GUESTS

Name: _____

Address: _____

_____

Relationship To Parents: _____

BABY PREDICTIONS

Date Of Birth: _____

Time Of Birth: _____

Baby Weight: _____

Baby Height: _____

Hair Color: _____

Eye Color: _____

First Word: _____

Resemblance: ☐ Mom ☐ Dad

I Hope The Baby Gets Dad's

_____

I Hope The Baby Gets Mom's

_____

WISHES FOR BABY

_____

_____

_____

ADVICE FOR PARENTS

_____

_____

_____

Thanks For Sharing

GUESTS

Name: _____

Address: _____

_____

Relationship To Parents: _____

BABY PREDICTIONS

Date Of Birth: _____

Time Of Birth: _____

Baby Weight: _____

Baby Height: _____

Hair Color: _____

Eye Color: _____

First Word: _____

Resemblance: ☐ Mom ☐ Dad

I Hope The Baby Gets Dad's

_____

_____

I Hope The Baby Gets Mom's

_____

_____

WISHES FOR BABY

_____

_____

_____

ADVICE FOR PARENTS

_____

_____

_____

Thanks For Sharing

GUESTS

Name: _____

Address: _____

_____

Relationship To Parents: _____

BABY PREDICTIONS

Date Of Birth: _____

Time Of Birth: _____

Baby Weight: _____

Baby Height: _____

Hair Color: _____

Eye Color: _____

First Word: _____

Resemblance: ☐ Mom ☐ Dad

I Hope The Baby Gets Dad's

_____

_____

I Hope The Baby Gets Mom's

_____

_____

WISHES FOR BABY

_____

_____

_____

ADVICE FOR PARENTS

_____

_____

_____

Thanks For Sharing

GUESTS

Name: _____

Address: _____

_____

Relationship To Parents: _____

BABY PREDICTIONS

Date Of Birth: _____

Time Of Birth: _____

Baby Weight: _____

Baby Height: _____

Hair Color: _____

Eye Color: _____

First Word: _____

Resemblance: ☐ Mom ☐ Dad

I Hope The Baby Gets Dad's

_____

_____

I Hope The Baby Gets Mom's

_____

_____

WISHES FOR BABY

_____

_____

_____

ADVICE FOR PARENTS

_____

_____

_____

Thanks For Sharing

GUESTS

Name: _____

Address: _____

_____

Relationship To Parents: _____

BABY PREDICTIONS

Date Of Birth: _____

Time Of Birth: _____

Baby Weight: _____

Baby Height: _____

Hair Color: _____

Eye Color: _____

First Word: _____

Resemblance: ☐ Mom ☐ Dad

I Hope The Baby Gets Dad's

_____

_____

I Hope The Baby Gets Mom's

_____

_____

WISHES FOR BABY

_____

_____

_____

ADVICE FOR PARENTS

_____

_____

_____

Thanks For Sharing

GUESTS

Name: _____

Address: _____

_____

Relationship To Parents: _____

BABY PREDICTIONS

Date Of Birth: _____

Time Of Birth: _____

Baby Weight: _____

Baby Height: _____

Hair Color: _____

Eye Color: _____

First Word: _____

Resemblance: ☐ Mom ☐ Dad

I Hope The Baby Gets Dad's

_____

_____

I Hope The Baby Gets Mom's

_____

_____

WISHES FOR BABY

_____

_____

_____

ADVICE FOR PARENTS

_____

_____

_____

Thanks For Sharing

GUESTS

Name: _____

Address: _____

_____

Relationship To Parents: _____

BABY PREDICTIONS

Date Of Birth: _____

Time Of Birth: _____

Baby Weight: _____

Baby Height: _____

Hair Color: _____

Eye Color: _____

First Word: _____

Resemblance: ☐ Mom ☐ Dad

I Hope The Baby Gets Dad's

_____

I Hope The Baby Gets Mom's

_____

WISHES FOR BABY

_____

_____

_____

ADVICE FOR PARENTS

_____

_____

_____

Thanks For Sharing

GUESTS

Name: _____

Address: _____

_____

Relationship To Parents: _____

BABY PREDICTIONS

Date Of Birth: _____

Time Of Birth: _____

Baby Weight: _____

Baby Height: _____

Hair Color: _____

Eye Color: _____

First Word: _____

Resemblance: ☐ Mom ☐ Dad

I Hope The Baby Gets Dad's

_____

I Hope The Baby Gets Mom's

_____

WISHES FOR BABY

_____

_____

_____

ADVICE FOR PARENTS

_____

_____

_____

Thanks For Sharing

GUESTS

Name: _____

Address: _____

_____

Relationship To Parents: _____

BABY PREDICTIONS

Date Of Birth: _____

Time Of Birth: _____

Baby Weight: _____

Baby Height: _____

Hair Color: _____

Eye Color: _____

First Word: _____

Resemblance: ☐ Mom ☐ Dad

I Hope The Baby Gets Dad's

_____

I Hope The Baby Gets Mom's

_____

WISHES FOR BABY

_____

_____

_____

ADVICE FOR PARENTS

_____

_____

_____

Thanks For Sharing

GUESTS

Name: _____

Address: _____

_____

Relationship To Parents: _____

BABY PREDICTIONS

Date Of Birth: _____

Time Of Birth: _____

Baby Weight: _____

Baby Height: _____

Hair Color: _____

Eye Color: _____

First Word: _____

Resemblance: ☐ Mom ☐ Dad

I Hope The Baby Gets Dad's

_____

_____

I Hope The Baby Gets Mom's

_____

_____

WISHES FOR BABY

_____

_____

_____

ADVICE FOR PARENTS

_____

_____

_____

Thanks For Sharing

GUESTS

Name: _____

Address: _____

_____

Relationship To Parents: _____

BABY PREDICTIONS

Date Of Birth: _____

Time Of Birth: _____

Baby Weight: _____

Baby Height: _____

Hair Color: _____

Eye Color: _____

First Word: _____

Resemblance: ☐ Mom ☐ Dad

I Hope The Baby Gets Dad's

_____

_____

I Hope The Baby Gets Mom's

_____

_____

WISHES FOR BABY

_____

_____

_____

ADVICE FOR PARENTS

_____

_____

Thanks For Sharing

GUESTS

Name: _____

Address: _____

_____

Relationship To Parents: _____

BABY PREDICTIONS

Date Of Birth: _____

Time Of Birth: _____

Baby Weight: _____

Baby Height: _____

Hair Color: _____

Eye Color: _____

First Word: _____

Resemblance: ☐ Mom ☐ Dad

I Hope The Baby Gets Dad's

_____

_____

I Hope The Baby Gets Mom's

_____

_____

WISHES FOR BABY

_____

_____

_____

ADVICE FOR PARENTS

_____

_____

_____

Thanks For Sharing

GUESTS

Name: _____

Address: _____

_____

Relationship To Parents: _____

BABY PREDICTIONS

Date Of Birth: _____

Time Of Birth: _____

Baby Weight: _____

Baby Height: _____

Hair Color: _____

Eye Color: _____

First Word: _____

Resemblance: ☐ Mom ☐ Dad

I Hope The Baby Gets Dad's

_____

I Hope The Baby Gets Mom's

_____

WISHES FOR BABY

_____

_____

_____

ADVICE FOR PARENTS

_____

_____

Thanks For Sharing

GUESTS

Name: _____

Address: _____

_____

Relationship To Parents: _____

BABY PREDICTIONS

Date Of Birth: _____

Time Of Birth: _____

Baby Weight: _____

Baby Height: _____

Hair Color: _____

Eye Color: _____

First Word: _____

Resemblance: ☐ Mom ☐ Dad

I Hope The Baby Gets Dad's

_____

_____

I Hope The Baby Gets Mom's

_____

_____

WISHES FOR BABY

_____

_____

_____

ADVICE FOR PARENTS

_____

_____

Thanks For Sharing

GUESTS

Name: _____

Address: _____

_____

Relationship To Parents: _____

BABY PREDICTIONS

Date Of Birth: _____

Time Of Birth: _____

Baby Weight: _____

Baby Height: _____

Hair Color: _____

Eye Color: _____

First Word: _____

Resemblance: ☐ Mom ☐ Dad

I Hope The Baby Gets Dad's

_____

_____

I Hope The Baby Gets Mom's

_____

_____

WISHES FOR BABY

_____

_____

_____

ADVICE FOR PARENTS

_____

_____

_____

Thanks For Sharing

GUESTS

Name: _____

Address: _____

_____

Relationship To Parents: _____

BABY PREDICTIONS

Date Of Birth: _____

Time Of Birth: _____

Baby Weight: _____

Baby Height: _____

Hair Color: _____

Eye Color: _____

First Word: _____

Resemblance: ☐ Mom ☐ Dad

I Hope The Baby Gets Dad's

_____

_____

I Hope The Baby Gets Mom's

_____

_____

WISHES FOR BABY

_____

_____

_____

ADVICE FOR PARENTS

_____

_____

Thanks For Sharing

GUESTS

Name: _____

Address: _____

_____

Relationship To Parents: _____

BABY PREDICTIONS

Date Of Birth: _____

Time Of Birth: _____

Baby Weight: _____

Baby Height: _____

Hair Color: _____

Eye Color: _____

First Word: _____

Resemblance: ☐ Mom ☐ Dad

I Hope The Baby Gets Dad's

_____

_____

I Hope The Baby Gets Mom's

_____

_____

WISHES FOR BABY

_____

_____

_____

ADVICE FOR PARENTS

_____

_____

Thanks For Sharing

GUESTS

Name: _____

Address: _____

_____

Relationship To Parents: _____

BABY PREDICTIONS

Date Of Birth: _____

Time Of Birth: _____

Baby Weight: _____

Baby Height: _____

Hair Color: _____

Eye Color: _____

First Word: _____

Resemblance: ☐ Mom ☐ Dad

I Hope The Baby Gets Dad's

_____

I Hope The Baby Gets Mom's

_____

WISHES FOR BABY

_____

_____

_____

ADVICE FOR PARENTS

_____

_____

_____

Thanks For Sharing

GUESTS

Name: _____

Address: _____

_____

Relationship To Parents: _____

BABY PREDICTIONS

Date Of Birth: _____

Time Of Birth: _____

Baby Weight: _____

Baby Height: _____

Hair Color: _____

Eye Color: _____

First Word: _____

Resemblance: ☐ Mom ☐ Dad

I Hope The Baby Gets Dad's

_____

I Hope The Baby Gets Mom's

_____

WISHES FOR BABY

_____

_____

_____

ADVICE FOR PARENTS

_____

_____

_____

Thanks For Sharing

GUESTS

Name: _____

Address: _____

_____

Relationship To Parents: _____

BABY PREDICTIONS

Date Of Birth: _____

Time Of Birth: _____

Baby Weight: _____

Baby Height: _____

Hair Color: _____

Eye Color: _____

First Word: _____

Resemblance: ☐Mom ☐Dad

I Hope The Baby Gets Dad's

_____

_____

I Hope The Baby Gets Mom's

_____

_____

WISHES FOR BABY

_____

_____

_____

ADVICE FOR PARENTS

_____

_____

Thanks For Sharing

GUESTS

Name: _____

Address: _____

_____

Relationship To Parents: _____

BABY PREDICTIONS

Date Of Birth: _____

Time Of Birth: _____

Baby Weight: _____

Baby Height: _____

Hair Color: _____

Eye Color: _____

First Word: _____

Resemblance: ☐ Mom ☐ Dad

I Hope The Baby Gets Dad's

_____

I Hope The Baby Gets Mom's

_____

WISHES FOR BABY

_____

_____

_____

ADVICE FOR PARENTS

_____

_____

_____

Thanks For Sharing

GUESTS

Name: _____

Address: _____

_____

Relationship To Parents: _____

BABY PREDICTIONS

Date Of Birth: _____

Time Of Birth: _____

Baby Weight: _____

Baby Height: _____

Hair Color: _____

Eye Color: _____

First Word: _____

Resemblance: ☐ Mom ☐ Dad

I Hope The Baby Gets Dad's

_____

_____

I Hope The Baby Gets Mom's

_____

_____

WISHES FOR BABY

_____

_____

_____

ADVICE FOR PARENTS

_____

_____

_____

Thanks For Sharing

GUESTS

Name: _____

Address: _____

_____

Relationship To Parents: _____

BABY PREDICTIONS

Date Of Birth: _____

Time Of Birth: _____

Baby Weight: _____

Baby Height: _____

Hair Color: _____

Eye Color: _____

First Word: _____

Resemblance: ☐ Mom ☐ Dad

I Hope The Baby Gets Dad's

_____

I Hope The Baby Gets Mom's

_____

WISHES FOR BABY

_____

_____

_____

ADVICE FOR PARENTS

_____

_____

_____

Thanks For Sharing

GUESTS

Name: _____

Address: _____

_____

Relationship To Parents: _____

BABY PREDICTIONS

Date Of Birth: _____   Resemblance: ☐ Mom ☐ Dad

Time Of Birth: _____   I Hope The Baby Gets Dad's

Baby Weight: _____

Baby Height: _____   _____

Hair Color: _____   I Hope The Baby Gets Mom's

Eye Color: _____

First Word: _____   _____

WISHES FOR BABY

_____

_____

_____

ADVICE FOR PARENTS

_____

_____

_____

Thanks For Sharing

GUESTS

Name: _____

Address: _____

_____

Relationship To Parents: _____

BABY PREDICTIONS

Date Of Birth: _____

Time Of Birth: _____

Baby Weight: _____

Baby Height: _____

Hair Color: _____

Eye Color: _____

First Word: _____

Resemblance: ☐ Mom ☐ Dad

I Hope The Baby Gets Dad's

_____

_____

I Hope The Baby Gets Mom's

_____

WISHES FOR BABY

_____

_____

_____

ADVICE FOR PARENTS

_____

_____

_____

Thanks For Sharing

GUESTS

Name: _____

Address: _____

_____

Relationship To Parents: _____

BABY PREDICTIONS

Date Of Birth: _____

Time Of Birth: _____

Baby Weight: _____

Baby Height: _____

Hair Color: _____

Eye Color: _____

First Word: _____

Resemblance: ☐ Mom ☐ Dad

I Hope The Baby Gets Dad's

_____

I Hope The Baby Gets Mom's

_____

WISHES FOR BABY

_____

_____

_____

ADVICE FOR PARENTS

_____

_____

_____

Thanks For Sharing

GUESTS

Name: _____

Address: _____

_____

Relationship To Parents: _____

BABY PREDICTIONS

Date Of Birth: _____

Time Of Birth: _____

Baby Weight: _____

Baby Height: _____

Hair Color: _____

Eye Color: _____

First Word: _____

Resemblance: ☐ Mom ☐ Dad

I Hope The Baby Gets Dad's

_____

_____

I Hope The Baby Gets Mom's

_____

_____

WISHES FOR BABY

_____

_____

_____

ADVICE FOR PARENTS

_____

_____

_____

Thanks For Sharing

GUESTS

Name: _____

Address: _____

_____

Relationship To Parents: _____

BABY PREDICTIONS

Date Of Birth: _____

Time Of Birth: _____

Baby Weight: _____

Baby Height: _____

Hair Color: _____

Eye Color: _____

First Word: _____

Resemblance: ☐ Mom ☐ Dad

I Hope The Baby Gets Dad's

_____

_____

I Hope The Baby Gets Mom's

_____

_____

WISHES FOR BABY

_____

_____

_____

ADVICE FOR PARENTS

_____

_____

_____

Thanks For Sharing

GUESTS

Name: _____

Address: _____

_____

Relationship To Parents: _____

BABY PREDICTIONS

Date Of Birth: _____

Time Of Birth: _____

Baby Weight: _____

Baby Height: _____

Hair Color: _____

Eye Color: _____

First Word: _____

Resemblance: ☐ Mom ☐ Dad

I Hope The Baby Gets Dad's

_____

_____

I Hope The Baby Gets Mom's

_____

_____

WISHES FOR BABY

_____

_____

_____

ADVICE FOR PARENTS

_____

_____

_____

Thanks For Sharing

GUESTS

Name: _____

Address: _____

_____

Relationship To Parents: _____

BABY PREDICTIONS

Date Of Birth: _____

Time Of Birth: _____

Baby Weight: _____

Baby Height: _____

Hair Color: _____

Eye Color: _____

First Word: _____

Resemblance: □ Mom □ Dad

I Hope The Baby Gets Dad's

_____

_____

I Hope The Baby Gets Mom's

_____

_____

WISHES FOR BABY

_____

_____

_____

ADVICE FOR PARENTS

_____

_____

_____

Thanks For Sharing

GUESTS

Name: _____

Address: _____

_____

Relationship To Parents: _____

BABY PREDICTIONS

Date Of Birth: _____

Time Of Birth: _____

Baby Weight: _____

Baby Height: _____

Hair Color: _____

Eye Color: _____

First Word: _____

Resemblance: ☐ Mom ☐ Dad

I Hope The Baby Gets Dad's

_____

_____

I Hope The Baby Gets Mom's

_____

_____

WISHES FOR BABY

_____

_____

_____

ADVICE FOR PARENTS

_____

_____

_____

Thanks For Sharing

GUESTS

Name: _____

Address: _____

_____

Relationship To Parents: _____

BABY PREDICTIONS

Date Of Birth: _____

Time Of Birth: _____

Baby Weight: _____

Baby Height: _____

Hair Color: _____

Eye Color: _____

First Word: _____

Resemblance: ☐ Mom ☐ Dad

I Hope The Baby Gets Dad's

_____

_____

I Hope The Baby Gets Mom's

_____

_____

WISHES FOR BABY

_____

_____

_____

ADVICE FOR PARENTS

_____

_____

_____

Thanks For Sharing

GUESTS

Name: _____

Address: _____

_____

Relationship To Parents: _____

BABY PREDICTIONS

Date Of Birth: _____

Time Of Birth: _____

Baby Weight: _____

Baby Height: _____

Hair Color: _____

Eye Color: _____

First Word: _____

Resemblance: ☐ Mom ☐ Dad

I Hope The Baby Gets Dad's

_____

_____

I Hope The Baby Gets Mom's

_____

_____

WISHES FOR BABY

_____

_____

_____

ADVICE FOR PARENTS

_____

_____

_____

Thanks For Sharing

GUESTS

Name: _____

Address: _____

_____

Relationship To Parents: _____

BABY PREDICTIONS

Date Of Birth: _____

Time Of Birth: _____

Baby Weight: _____

Baby Height: _____

Hair Color: _____

Eye Color: _____

First Word: _____

Resemblance: ☐Mom ☐Dad

I Hope The Baby Gets Dad's

_____

_____

I Hope The Baby Gets Mom's

_____

WISHES FOR BABY

_____

_____

_____

ADVICE FOR PARENTS

_____

_____

Thanks For Sharing

GUESTS

Name: _____

Address: _____

_____

Relationship To Parents: _____

BABY PREDICTIONS

Date Of Birth: _____

Time Of Birth: _____

Baby Weight: _____

Baby Height: _____

Hair Color: _____

Eye Color: _____

First Word: _____

Resemblance: ☐ Mom ☐ Dad

I Hope The Baby Gets Dad's

_____

_____

I Hope The Baby Gets Mom's

_____

_____

WISHES FOR BABY

_____

_____

_____

ADVICE FOR PARENTS

_____

_____

_____

Thanks For Sharing

GUESTS

Name: _____

Address: _____

_____

Relationship To Parents: _____

BABY PREDICTIONS

Date Of Birth: _____

Time Of Birth: _____

Baby Weight: _____

Baby Height: _____

Hair Color: _____

Eye Color: _____

First Word: _____

Resemblance: ☐Mom ☐Dad

I Hope The Baby Gets Dad's

_____

_____

I Hope The Baby Gets Mom's

_____

_____

WISHES FOR BABY

_____

_____

_____

ADVICE FOR PARENTS

_____

_____

_____

Thanks For Sharing

GUESTS

Name: _____

Address: _____

_____

Relationship To Parents: _____

BABY PREDICTIONS

Date Of Birth: _____

Time Of Birth: _____

Baby Weight: _____

Baby Height: _____

Hair Color: _____

Eye Color: _____

First Word: _____

Resemblance: ☐ Mom ☐ Dad

I Hope The Baby Gets Dad's

_____

I Hope The Baby Gets Mom's

_____

WISHES FOR BABY

_____

_____

_____

ADVICE FOR PARENTS

_____

_____

Thanks For Sharing

GUESTS

Name: _____

Address: _____

_____

Relationship To Parents: _____

BABY PREDICTIONS

Date Of Birth: _____

Time Of Birth: _____

Baby Weight: _____

Baby Height: _____

Hair Color: _____

Eye Color: _____

First Word: _____

Resemblance: ☐ Mom ☐ Dad

I Hope The Baby Gets Dad's

_____

_____

I Hope The Baby Gets Mom's

_____

WISHES FOR BABY

_____

_____

_____

ADVICE FOR PARENTS

_____

_____

Thanks For Sharing

GUESTS

Name: _____

Address: _____

_____

Relationship To Parents: _____

BABY PREDICTIONS

Date Of Birth: _____

Time Of Birth: _____

Baby Weight: _____

Baby Height: _____

Hair Color: _____

Eye Color: _____

First Word: _____

Resemblance: ☐ Mom ☐ Dad

I Hope The Baby Gets Dad's

_____

_____

I Hope The Baby Gets Mom's

_____

WISHES FOR BABY

_____

_____

_____

ADVICE FOR PARENTS

_____

_____

_____

Thanks For Sharing

GUESTS

Name: _____

Address: _____

_____

Relationship To Parents: _____

BABY PREDICTIONS

Date Of Birth: _____

Time Of Birth: _____

Baby Weight: _____

Baby Height: _____

Hair Color: _____

Eye Color: _____

First Word: _____

Resemblance: ☐ Mom ☐ Dad

I Hope The Baby Gets Dad's

_____

_____

I Hope The Baby Gets Mom's

_____

_____

WISHES FOR BABY

_____

_____

_____

ADVICE FOR PARENTS

_____

_____

_____

Thanks For Sharing

GUESTS

Name: _____

Address: _____

_____

Relationship To Parents: _____

BABY PREDICTIONS

Date Of Birth: _____

Time Of Birth: _____

Baby Weight: _____

Baby Height: _____

Hair Color: _____

Eye Color: _____

First Word: _____

Resemblance: ☐ Mom ☐ Dad

I Hope The Baby Gets Dad's

_____

_____

I Hope The Baby Gets Mom's

_____

_____

WISHES FOR BABY

_____

_____

_____

ADVICE FOR PARENTS

_____

_____

_____

Thanks For Sharing

GUESTS

Name: _____

Address: _____

_____

Relationship To Parents: _____

BABY PREDICTIONS

Date Of Birth: _____

Time Of Birth: _____

Baby Weight: _____

Baby Height: _____

Hair Color: _____

Eye Color: _____

First Word: _____

Resemblance: ☐ Mom ☐ Dad

I Hope The Baby Gets Dad's

_____

_____

I Hope The Baby Gets Mom's

_____

_____

WISHES FOR BABY

_____

_____

_____

ADVICE FOR PARENTS

_____

_____

_____

Thanks For Sharing

GUESTS

Name: _____

Address: _____

_____

Relationship To Parents: _____

BABY PREDICTIONS

Date Of Birth: _____

Time Of Birth: _____

Baby Weight: _____

Baby Height: _____

Hair Color: _____

Eye Color: _____

First Word: _____

Resemblance: ☐ Mom ☐ Dad

I Hope The Baby Gets Dad's

_____

_____

I Hope The Baby Gets Mom's

_____

_____

WISHES FOR BABY

_____

_____

_____

ADVICE FOR PARENTS

_____

_____

_____

Thanks For Sharing

GUESTS

Name: _____

Address: _____

_____

Relationship To Parents: _____

BABY PREDICTIONS

Date Of Birth: _____

Time Of Birth: _____

Baby Weight: _____

Baby Height: _____

Hair Color: _____

Eye Color: _____

First Word: _____

Resemblance: ☐ Mom ☐ Dad

I Hope The Baby Gets Dad's

_____

_____

I Hope The Baby Gets Mom's

_____

_____

WISHES FOR BABY

_____

_____

_____

ADVICE FOR PARENTS

_____

_____

_____

Thanks For Sharing

GUESTS

Name: _____

Address: _____

_____

Relationship To Parents: _____

BABY PREDICTIONS

Date Of Birth: _____

Time Of Birth: _____

Baby Weight: _____

Baby Height: _____

Hair Color: _____

Eye Color: _____

First Word: _____

Resemblance: ☐ Mom ☐ Dad

I Hope The Baby Gets Dad's

_____

_____

I Hope The Baby Gets Mom's

_____

_____

WISHES FOR BABY

_____

_____

_____

ADVICE FOR PARENTS

_____

_____

_____

Thanks For Sharing

GUESTS

Name: _____

Address: _____

_____

Relationship To Parents: _____

BABY PREDICTIONS

Date Of Birth: _____

Time Of Birth: _____

Baby Weight: _____

Baby Height: _____

Hair Color: _____

Eye Color: _____

First Word: _____

Resemblance: ☐ Mom ☐ Dad

I Hope The Baby Gets Dad's

_____

_____

I Hope The Baby Gets Mom's

_____

_____

WISHES FOR BABY

_____

_____

_____

ADVICE FOR PARENTS

_____

_____

_____

Thanks For Sharing

GUESTS

Name: _____

Address: _____

_____

Relationship To Parents: _____

BABY PREDICTIONS

Date Of Birth: _____

Time Of Birth: _____

Baby Weight: _____

Baby Height: _____

Hair Color: _____

Eye Color: _____

First Word: _____

Resemblance: ☐ Mom ☐ Dad

I Hope The Baby Gets Dad's

_____

_____

I Hope The Baby Gets Mom's

_____

_____

WISHES FOR BABY

_____

_____

_____

ADVICE FOR PARENTS

_____

_____

_____

Thanks For Sharing

GUESTS

Name: _____

Address: _____

_____

Relationship To Parents: _____

BABY PREDICTIONS

Date Of Birth: _____

Time Of Birth: _____

Baby Weight: _____

Baby Height: _____

Hair Color: _____

Eye Color: _____

First Word: _____

Resemblance: ☐ Mom ☐ Dad

I Hope The Baby Gets Dad's

_____

_____

I Hope The Baby Gets Mom's

_____

_____

WISHES FOR BABY

_____

_____

_____

ADVICE FOR PARENTS

_____

_____

Thanks For Sharing

GUESTS

Name: _____

Address: _____

_____

Relationship To Parents: _____

BABY PREDICTIONS

Date Of Birth: _____

Time Of Birth: _____

Baby Weight: _____

Baby Height: _____

Hair Color: _____

Eye Color: _____

First Word: _____

Resemblance: ☐ Mom ☐ Dad

I Hope The Baby Gets Dad's

_____

_____

I Hope The Baby Gets Mom's

_____

WISHES FOR BABY

_____

_____

_____

ADVICE FOR PARENTS

_____

_____

_____

Thanks For Sharing

GUESTS

Name: _____

Address: _____

_____

Relationship To Parents: _____

BABY PREDICTIONS

Date Of Birth: _____

Time Of Birth: _____

Baby Weight: _____

Baby Height: _____

Hair Color: _____

Eye Color: _____

First Word: _____

Resemblance: ☐ Mom ☐ Dad

I Hope The Baby Gets Dad's

_____

_____

I Hope The Baby Gets Mom's

_____

_____

WISHES FOR BABY

_____

_____

_____

ADVICE FOR PARENTS

_____

_____

Thanks For Sharing

GUESTS

Name: _____

Address: _____

_____

Relationship To Parents: _____

BABY PREDICTIONS

Date Of Birth: _____

Time Of Birth: _____

Baby Weight: _____

Baby Height: _____

Hair Color: _____

Eye Color: _____

First Word: _____

Resemblance: ☐Mom ☐Dad

I Hope The Baby Gets Dad's

_____

_____

I Hope The Baby Gets Mom's

_____

WISHES FOR BABY

_____

_____

_____

ADVICE FOR PARENTS

_____

_____

_____

Thanks For Sharing

GUESTS

Name: _____

Address: _____

_____

Relationship To Parents: _____

BABY PREDICTIONS

Date Of Birth: _____

Time Of Birth: _____

Baby Weight: _____

Baby Height: _____

Hair Color: _____

Eye Color: _____

First Word: _____

Resemblance: ☐ Mom ☐ Dad

I Hope The Baby Gets Dad's

_____

I Hope The Baby Gets Mom's

_____

WISHES FOR BABY

_____

_____

_____

ADVICE FOR PARENTS

_____

_____

_____

Thanks For Sharing

GUESTS

Name: _____

Address: _____

_____

Relationship To Parents: _____

BABY PREDICTIONS

Date Of Birth: _____

Time Of Birth: _____

Baby Weight: _____

Baby Height: _____

Hair Color: _____

Eye Color: _____

First Word: _____

Resemblance: ☐ Mom ☐ Dad

I Hope The Baby Gets Dad's

_____

_____

I Hope The Baby Gets Mom's

_____

_____

WISHES FOR BABY

_____

_____

_____

ADVICE FOR PARENTS

_____

_____

_____

Thanks For Sharing

GUESTS

Name: _____

Address: _____

_____

Relationship To Parents: _____

BABY PREDICTIONS

Date Of Birth: _____

Time Of Birth: _____

Baby Weight: _____

Baby Height: _____

Hair Color: _____

Eye Color: _____

First Word: _____

Resemblance: ☐ Mom ☐ Dad

I Hope The Baby Gets Dad's

_____

_____

I Hope The Baby Gets Mom's

_____

WISHES FOR BABY

_____

_____

_____

ADVICE FOR PARENTS

_____

_____

_____

Thanks For Sharing

GUESTS

Name: _____

Address: _____

_____

Relationship To Parents: _____

BABY PREDICTIONS

Date Of Birth: _____

Time Of Birth: _____

Baby Weight: _____

Baby Height: _____

Hair Color: _____

Eye Color: _____

First Word: _____

Resemblance: ☐ Mom ☐ Dad

I Hope The Baby Gets Dad's

_____

_____

I Hope The Baby Gets Mom's

_____

_____

WISHES FOR BABY

_____

_____

_____

ADVICE FOR PARENTS

_____

_____

_____

Thanks For Sharing

GUESTS

Name: _____

Address: _____

_____

Relationship To Parents: _____

BABY PREDICTIONS

Date Of Birth: _____

Time Of Birth: _____

Baby Weight: _____

Baby Height: _____

Hair Color: _____

Eye Color: _____

First Word: _____

Resemblance: ☐ Mom ☐ Dad

I Hope The Baby Gets Dad's

_____

_____

I Hope The Baby Gets Mom's

_____

WISHES FOR BABY

_____

_____

_____

ADVICE FOR PARENTS

_____

_____

_____

Thanks For Sharing

GUESTS

Name: _____

Address: _____

_____

Relationship To Parents: _____

BABY PREDICTIONS

Date Of Birth: _____

Time Of Birth: _____

Baby Weight: _____

Baby Height: _____

Hair Color: _____

Eye Color: _____

First Word: _____

Resemblance: ☐ Mom ☐ Dad

I Hope The Baby Gets Dad's

_____

_____

I Hope The Baby Gets Mom's

_____

_____

WISHES FOR BABY

_____

_____

_____

ADVICE FOR PARENTS

_____

_____

_____

Thanks For Sharing

GUESTS

Name: _____

Address: _____

_____

Relationship To Parents: _____

BABY PREDICTIONS

Date Of Birth: _____

Time Of Birth: _____

Baby Weight: _____

Baby Height: _____

Hair Color: _____

Eye Color: _____

First Word: _____

Resemblance: ☐ Mom ☐ Dad

I Hope The Baby Gets Dad's

_____

_____

I Hope The Baby Gets Mom's

_____

_____

WISHES FOR BABY

_____

_____

_____

ADVICE FOR PARENTS

_____

_____

_____

Thanks For Sharing

GIFT LOG

Gift Received	Given By	Thank You?

GIFT LOG

Gift Received	Given By	Thank You?

GIFT LOG

Gift Received	Given By	Thank You?

GIFT LOG

Gift Received	Given By	Thank You?

GIFT LOG

Gift Received	Given By	Thank You?

NOTES

NOTES

NOTES

NOTES

9ae0e558-873a-43f6-8415-1ecd1cc5e878R01